Randle B. Truett.

THE First Ladies in Fashion

THE
First Ladies
in Fashion

BY

RANDLE BOND TRUETT

WITH FASHION NOTES BY

PHILIP ROBERTSON
COUTURIER, WASHINGTON, D. C.

HASTINGS HOUSE, PUBLISHERS

NEW YORK

ACKNOWLEDGMENTS

I wish to express my appreciation to the Smithsonian Institution for making available the photographs of the gowns included in their "Collection of Dresses of the First Ladies of the White House." Special thanks go to Miss Margaret W. Brown, Associate Curator, Department of History, Smithsonian Institution, for her assistance. Miss Brown is in charge of the maintenance and development of the Collection and is the author of the Smithsonian Publication entitled *The Dresses of the First Ladies of the White House*, with 35 color plates, published in 1952, which was exceedingly helpful in the compilation of this book. My sincere thanks go also to Frank Turgeon, Jr., A.R.P.S., for the use of his copyrighted direct color portrait of Mrs. Dwight D. Eisenhower. The descriptions of the gowns would have lacked the professional touch of the couturier had not Philip Robertson written the fashion notes. He was assisted in this by Lucie Eberly.

R. B. T.

Introduction

*T*HE White House, as the focal political center of the nation, has always more or less set the pattern of practices and procedures for formal, official entertaining. Consequently the First Lady, because of her position as hostess in the Executive Mansion, has inevitably established certain fashion standards which have been accepted and generally followed by American women. One of the best cross sections of American period costume may be had from the Collection of Dresses of the First Ladies of the White House which is on permanent display in the Arts and Industries Building of the Smithsonian Institution in Washington, D. C. In order that the coverage should be entirely up-to-date, Mrs. Dwight D. Eisenhower's inaugural ball gown has been included, as well as being reproduced on the jacket. In November, 1953, Mrs. Eisenhower announced that she was sending to the Smithsonian Institution her Inaugural Ball gown to represent her in the Collection. Whereupon it was decided by the Institution to place the gown on display while she was still in the White House rather than wait until the close of her husband's administration. The 37 gowns now in the Collection represent the changes in fashion in this country over a period of 164 years, from the administration of George Washington to the present administration.

This exceedingly popular and famous costume group had its inception about 50 years ago. Mrs. Julian James of Washington, D. C. believed that such a display, housed in the Smithsonian Institution, would be both interesting and of definite educational value. Mrs. Rose Gouverneur Hoes soon joined with Mrs. James to organize the Collection. Mrs. Hoes, a descendant of President James Monroe, had in her possession many of the Monroe heirlooms, including several costumes of the family. With this start, the potentialities of such a project caught the imagination of many prominent people. One of the first to present a gown to the Collection was Mrs. William Howard Taft, at that time, 1912, First Lady of the White House. Former First Ladies or their descendants all over the United States were approached and asked to supplement the growing Collection. There followed in rapid succession the presentation of more dresses. Only a comparatively short period of time elapsed before the entire group was successfully assembled, and this rapid accomplishment of an apparently difficult project must be attributed to a great extent to Mrs. Taft's immediate and enthusiastic co-operation and interest. As the dresses began to come in the problem that arose in connection with their display had to be considered. A hall in the Arts and Industries Building of the Smithsonian was designed for this purpose. Each gown as it was received was placed on a specially designed plaster figure. It was agreed that it would not be practical to attempt to model each head

5

individually but rather to use a standard head, one done by Pierce F. Connelly, sculptor, of Lousiana. Minor modifications were made by changing the expression of the eyes and the method of dressing the hair; the coiffure in each case was copied from a photograph, painting, or a piece of statuary of the First Lady who had worn the particular gown exhibited in the Collection. By this simple expedient a varied and interesting appearance, even though there was no attempt at portraiture, was given to the entire group.

There was another point that required consideration. At various times someone other than the wife of a President had acted as First Lady of the White House. This situation had arisen when the President was a widower or a bachelor or when the health of his wife would not permit her to act in her official capacity. On these occasions it was customary to invite a close relative or a family friend to serve as hostess for the administration. The costume committee finally decided that the Collection would be composed only of gowns worn by those who had been officially designated as hostesses for the Presidents.

The Collection vividly connotes social life in the White House during various epochs. The visitor regarding these brilliantly costumed figures can easily visualize a reception in the Blue Room, with the First Lady, in the graceful costume of Dolly Madison or the hoop skirts of Angelica Van Buren, or the royal-purple velvet gown worn by Mary Todd Lincoln, standing beside the President and receiving distinguished guests; or imagine her, at a more informal reception, greeting her friends in the East Room. The Collection gives color and substance to the prosaic record of the printed page by displaying types of materials and forms of decoration no longer in vogue, and, moreover, provides an excellent sampling of the fashion trends of the nation from the beginning down to our own day.

These dresses have a very wide appeal: they help history students complete the picture of particular periods; to the costume designer they furnish accurate examples of gowns worn during every administration since the establishment of the nation; to the doll collector they furnish perfect models for reproduction; to the art student they provide styles, designs and motifs; and to all of us, young and old, they make the First Ladies of the White House live again in a way that no other source material can.

THE
First Ladies
in Fashion

MARTHA WASHINGTON

*A*S the First Lady of the United States, Martha Washington served as official hostess for her husband, George Washington, from 1789 to 1797. The Executive Mansion during this period was first in New York and later in Philadelphia, for Washington, D. C. was at that time in the planning and building stages. Martha's family background and training enabled her to establish the duties and responsibilities of the newly created position which would be studied and followed by succeeding First Ladies. She realized that the attention of the entire nation, small as it then was, was focused on the home of its President. Martha Washington was determined that her weekly receptions and other state affairs should have an air of dignity but without pomp and ceremony. Her long experience at Mount Vernon as the charming wife of the country squire was an excellent preparation for the position she assumed as First Lady. It was her custom to be seated when receiving guests, and it is in this position that we find her represented in the Collection at the Smithsonian.

THE GOWN WORN by Martha Washington is typical of the late eighteenth century in both design and workmanship. It is fashioned of a salmon-pink hand-painted brocade; the pattern is made up of grey and white ribbon chains which form six-sided spaces caught together with emerald-green squares. In the center of the larger figures are painted clusters of morning-glories, violets, daisies, and buttercups with butterflies and bees in the squares. Edging the deep square neckline of the basque bodice is a band of fine ivory lace an inch wide. The waistline of the bodice comes to points in both front and back and is fastened in the back by hand lacing. From under the waistline of the bodice the skirt falls in deep unpressed pleats and gracefully sweeps the floor. The triangular shawl around the shoulders of the figure is of Mechlin lace, as are the short handmade mitts. Since Mrs. Washington always wore a "mobcap" to social affairs the costume has been completed with one of fine handmade lace ending in a full ruffle around the hairline and tied with a wide satin ribbon. Placed on her lap is a brown satin drawstring bag which she had embroidered with ribbonwork, forming a wreath of flowers encircling the name "Mrs. Washington" in old script.

ABIGAIL ADAMS

ABIGAIL ADAMS followed Martha Washington as hostess in Philadelphia, then the nation's capital, during her husband's administration from 1797 to 1801. The last few months of the administration of John Adams, however, were spent in the newly established capital, Washington, D. C. He and Abigail moved into the partially completed White House, then known as the President's House. She was a prolific letter writer and from these personal acounts we are able to visualize the almost rural condition existing in Washington when they arrived there. The first official gathering in the new surroundings was the New Year's Day reception. After having entertained at her home in Quincy, Massachusetts and later in Philadelphia, it must have been difficult for Abigail to organize a social season in a so-recently developed community and in a house that was far from completion. But as the First Lady of the White House, she rose nobly to the demands of her position though she did complain privately about the shortcomings of the unfinished Executive Mansion.

A SAPPHIRE-BLUE GOWN of heavy Canton crepe was selected to represent Abigail Adams. The daytime gown features a tightly fitted and boned bodice with interesting detail. Five diagonal tucks of matching satin run from the shoulder seams of the bodice to the point of the basque waistline in front, and from the sloping shoulders the sleeves are luxuriously shirred to the middle of the upper arm and are bound in satin. From this point leg-of-mutton sleeves fall to the wrist and are trimmed with small Mechlin lace cuffs. The V-shaped neckline is draped with a fichu of Mechlin lace and is pinned in front with a brooch of gold and pearls and then falls into a jabot. The straight-cut floor length skirt shirred to the satin-bound waist is made of the same Canton crepe and features a twenty-inch border of Chinese embroidery. The silk floss of the embroidery matches the crepe in color. As was typical of the era, the skirt was lined with crinoline to the top of the embroidery. A fan belonging to Mrs. Adams, in shades of blue and embroidered with tiny silver sequins, accompanies the gown, as do yellow kid heelless slippers.

W HEN Thomas Jefferson went to Washington as President, he was without an official hostess since his wife had died many years previously. During his administration several women acted as First Lady; among them was Dolly Madison, wife of the Secretary of State, who presided at many of the state dinners. But for much of the time President Jefferson's daughter, Martha, who was married to her cousin, Thomas Mann Randolph, acted as hostess for him. Martha was well qualified for her new duties, since she had been with her father during the years of his diplomatic mission in France and had acquired some experience of formal social life in the French capital. Her earlier associations stood her in good stead when called upon to preside at state functions. During Jefferson's presidency social entertainments at the White House were less formal than during the preceding administrations, and consequently the youthful Martha's responsibilities were not too onerous. When her father retired to Monticello, she continued to act as hostess for him, no easy role since hospitality was on a lavish scale and occasionally as many as fifty guests at a time were entertained there.

THE RANDOLPH FAMILY was not able to locate a gown belonging to Martha, for her dresses had disappeared; perhaps some of them were destroyed during the Civil War. But the search did produce one of her shawls, and it has been placed in the Collection to represent her. It is made of fine black wool and measures about eight by four feet. A wide paisley border with the typical cone pattern bands two sides of the shawl. The paisley is predominantly beige and brown and has subdued shades of blues, reds and greens woven through. The other two sides have a two-inch paisley braid binding the edge. Oriental shawls began to appear in Europe in the first part of the nineteenth century, and soon became the height of fashion in America.

DOLLY MADISON

*V*IVACIOUS Dolly Madison was First Lady from 1809 to 1817, when her husband, James Madison, was President. The experience as part-time hostess for Jefferson had been an excellent preparation for her new role. Her dinners and receptions were more elaborate than had been customary, but her talent for making people feel welcome despite all formalities made her one of the most popular of our First Ladies. The gay festivities Dolly had inaugurated were brought to an abrupt halt in 1814 when she had to flee from before the invading British army. Fortunately she managed to rescue the great Stuart portrait of Washington which today hangs in the East Room. On her return, with the White House a mass of ruins, she courageously reëstablished the social season in the Octagon House, temporary Executive Mansion. The administration came to a close in a blaze of glory with her last brilliant levee in the rebuilt White House, in February, 1816. She and Madison then retired to their home, Montpelier, where they continued to entertain on a grand scale. After his death Dolly again took up residence in Washington, and her occasional receptions were as crowded as those at the White House. She died at the ripe old age of seventy-seven.

THE GOWN OF Dolly Madison is what we today would classify as a "redingote" but in the early nineteenth century it was called a "sacque" dress. It is fashioned of an exquisite shade of golden-yellow Chinese silk brocade with a woven wheat spray motif of black, white, and silver. The tight, boned bodice has a wide off-shoulder boat neckline and ends short at the waist with a deep pointed Vee in front, emphasizing the early Empire waistline. The elbow-length sleeves are of puckered silk gauze and are fastened to satin under-sleeves and caught with tiny yellow pique-edged satin ribbon bowknots. The overskirt, open down the front, falls into deep folds at the waistline, is slightly draped, and ends in a short sweeping train. The shirred back of the overskirt gives a slight bustle effect. Around the entire edge of the overskirt is a full ruffle of Valenciennes lace. Underneath the redingote is a full skirt made of heavy white satin embroidered with delicate Chinese tracings of wild roses, cherry blossoms, and forget-me-nots, which form a scroll design down the front panel. A three-cornered stole of delicate Mechlin lace covers the caps of the shoulders. A band of satin which wrapped the head was an outstanding feature of Mrs. Madison's dress and was always worn at official functions.

ELIZABETH MONROE

*J*AMES MONROE and his beautiful wife, Elizabeth, in 1817 moved into the White House which had been rebuilt and which they helped refurnish. Their taste ran to French styles, since they had spent many years in France while Madison was American Minister there. They accordingly imported most of the furniture, silver and ornaments from Paris. The few pieces of Monroe furniture still in the White House are highly prized. The years of foreign residence, especially in Paris during the "terror" of the French Revolution, when Mrs. Monroe heroically intervened to save Madame de Lafayette from the guillotine, may have affected Mrs. Monroe's health. At any rate she failed to carry on the elaborate entertainment schedule established by Dolly Madison. The contrast between the social brilliance of the preceding regime and Elizabeth's more sober one seems to have adversely affected public opinion. Some unpopularity also resulted from Mrs. Monroe's modification and changes of certain White House customs to accord with the more formal style of entertaining prevalent in European capitals. But this tempest in a teapot soon subsided. The most spectacular event of Monroe's second term was the reception for Lafayette on his return to the United States in 1825. Then, after eight years in the White House, the Monroes were glad to retire to Oak Hill, their Virginia home.

THE COLORS IN the gown worn by Mrs. Monroe have not mellowed or faded through the last five generations. The heavy deep cream taffeta brocade has retained the brilliance in hues of the blood-red, yellow, and wine woven roses. This gown, much like that of Dolly Madison, was made along redingote lines. The suspender-like panels of ivory Point de Venise lace, which frames the neckline and ends at the waist, is filled in with vertically tucked cream-colored silk gauze, and the top is bound by a band of narrow lace. This "dicky" forms a square neckline. The elbow-length sleeves end in a cascade of finely pleated lawn edged with a narrow band of net. The Watteau back is one of the features of the gown. A deep inverted pleat

16   ELIZABETH MONROE

falls from the back of the neck, over the fitted waistline and into the skirt. The underskirt made of the same brocade has a wide ruffled flounce around the hem. Down the side fronts of the overskirt are appliqued scrolls of brocade with scattered tufts that give the effect of covered buttons. "Fly-fringe," which was commonly known as the outstanding trimming during the eighteenth century, is used around the sleeve ruffling and on the appliquéing of the gown. A heavy topaz necklace, which was a gift from President Monroe when he was Minister to France, is worn with the gown. The jewel, blending perfectly with the gown, is made up of eighteen oval shaped stones mounted in gold. A cross pendant is formed by five smaller stones, and there are two pear-shaped stones, also pendant, on either side of the cross.

ELIZABETH MONROE   17

*T*HOUGH only fourteen when her father, James Monroe, became President, Maria was already developing rapidly into a beautiful young woman and assisted her mother on many occasions. Within three short years of her father's election Maria was married to her cousin, Samuel Lawrence Gouverneur, who was at the time serving as a private secretary to the President and living at the White House. To Maria went the honor of being the first daughter of a President to be married in the Executive Mansion. Quite naturally all of Washington was absorbed in the plans for the forthcoming social event to which, however, only relatives and very close friends were invited. This did not diminsh the general interest in the wedding which was referred to in many contemporary letters and diaries. The exclusion of Washington society from the ceremony was resented by some, and the large reception given later by the Monroes for the young couple, followed by an elaborate ball under the auspices of Commodore and Mrs. Decatur, did not altogether appease public sentiment. In 1825, at the end of the administration, Maria and her husband went to New York to live. After the death of his wife, at Oak Hill, in Virginia, James Monroe made his home with his daughter, and her devoted attention was the solace of his declining years.

ONE OF THE smallest gowns in the Collection is that once worn by Maria, daughter of President Monroe. This gown was made in Paris in 1824 and is of sky-blue silk taffeta, fashioned along late Empire lines. It features a Watteau back as does the gown of her mother. The long basque waist has two panels down the front edged in yellow braid. The vertical lines of the panels run into a point over the skirt and are filled in with horizontal bands of embroidered taffeta, also edged

in yellow braid. The square neckline slopes out on the shoulders. Small puff sleeves of tulle are caught with bowknots of yellow and blue satin ribbons. There are two skirts, one over the other, and the outer one is shirred and puffed at the hipline, shortening it so that the hemline of the underskirt is seen. The scalloped hemlines of both skirts are heavily embroidered with straw, in a scroll wheat pattern. The straw floss was made by splitting the straw of ordinary wheat, and the embroidery technique gives it the appearance of silk. The edge of the taffeta is finished much like the lace flouncing in use today. It is interesting to note that the straw embroidery has been seen recently in modern fabrics.

MARIA GOUVERNEUR   19

LOUISA ADAMS

*I*N 1825 John Quincy Adams, second of the Adams clan to occupy that high post, came to the White House as President, bringing with him his London-born wife, Louisa, as First Lady. John Quincy's mother, Abigail Adams, had in her day complained because the Executive Mansion was not completed when she moved into it. Louisa found it still unfinished. The South Portico had just been added, but the North Portico was built during John Quincy's administration. Louisa did her share of official entertaining, but her health was frail. She had suffered from the severe winter climate while in Moscow with her husband during his service there as American Minister to Russia. Nevertheless, she enjoyed the social life of the Russian Capital, and had been thrilled when the Czar himself walked a Polonaise with her at the French Ambassador's ball. Her health suffered further on the long, hazardous journey through war-torn Europe to join her husband in Paris during the Hundred Days after Napoleon's return from Elba. John Quincy's administration proved to be a stormy one. But Louisa played her part with dignity and graciousness. Then the sudden death of their eldest son brought on a severe illness which lasted for weeks. She finally recovered sufficiently to preside at the reception, in December 1829, for Andrew Jackson, elected to succeed her husband. The Adamses returned to Washington after John Quincy's term was over and resided there on and off for twenty years more, while he served as Representative from Massachusetts. He was stricken down in 1848 as he rose to make a speech in the House. Louisa survived him by four years.

BY THE TIME Louisa Adams became the nation's First Lady in 1825 the Empire gown was at its height. Her gown is of white French illusion over heavy white silk satin. The low round neckline is edged with a ruching of illusion and delicate silver braid. Small puff sleeves are set into the sloped shoulder line and are decorated with the same braid as that used on the neckline.. Silver braid also girdles the high waistline, slightly under the bustline, and is caught to one side with satin

ribbon bows. The skirt is bell shaped and escapes the floor which allows the tips of the heelless satin slippers to show. The bottom of the skirt is heavily embossed with two rows of scallops of satin rope twisted with silver braid, and each cascade is caught with a satin and silver bow. Between the rows of rope scalloping are rows of ruching made with fluting of illusion, which is edged with silver filigree braid. The bottom of the hem is finished with a heavy satin and silver roping about an inch and a half in diameter, which acts as a hoop, holding the skirt out in a circular shape. The handkerchief in her hand is large in size, but the delicate fabric and fine embroidery make it extremely feminine.

EMILY DONELSON

*T*HE sudden death of Andrew Jackson's beloved wife, Rachel, only a few months before his inauguration left the position of First Lady without an incumbent. Andrew Jackson Donelson, for many years a ward of Andrew Jackson, married his cousin, Emily Donelson. They spent some time in Washington with Rachel and Andrew Jackson, then a Senator. Later when Jackson returned to Washington as President the Donelsons accompanied him, for Emily was to act as First Lady. Though only twenty-one she faced her new responsibilities in a manner that would have done credit to a more mature woman, and bore herself in her difficult position as White House hostess so well that she won general approval. Between her and the President there was always cordial understanding, except when the storm over Peggy O'Neal Eaton came to a head. Emily did not approve of Peggy, certainly did not consider her as an acceptable member of official White House society. So in 1830 she went to her home in Tennessee, there to remain until the next year when she returned and resumed her position as First Lady until 1836, when she became ill, victim of tuberculosis, which caused her death within the year.

THE GOWN ONCE worn by Emily Donelson is of gold brocade and lace. The basque bodice has off-shoulder neckline with a brocaded bertha collar edged with self binding. A garland of French illusion softens the neckline and is caught together in front and over the shoulders with dainty nosegays of flowers which match the rambling rose and violet pattern of the brocade. Tiny tucked sleeves peer from under the edge of the bertha collar, and falling from the edge of the sleeves is an elbow-length lace ruffle. From under the pointed basque waistline falls a soft ivory lace skirt over satin. From under the lace flounce extends another lace flounce to the edge of the hemline. Garlands of illusion caught with nosegays are repeated at the top of the lower skirt flouncing. The original skirt to this gown was destroyed in an accident before it could be placed in the Collection, therefore the lace skirt was added. The lace of which the skirt is made belonged to Mrs. Andrew Jackson. The hair style of this era was most extreme, piled high on top of the head in large puffs from which the upswept style of the mid-1940's was adapted.

SARAH JACKSON

*T*HE illness of Emily Donelson made it necessary for Sarah Jackson to come to Washington to assume the role of First Lady and preside at the White House. Sarah had married Andrew Jackson, Jr., the President's adopted son, a few years earlier. The young Jacksons had visited in the White House after the wedding and had been given a taste of the society that centers around the Chief Executive. They then returned to Tennessee and the Hermitage where Sarah presided as mistress for the rest of her life. There was never any question of the status of the two girls so long as Emily Donelson lived; Emily was First Lady at the White House and Sarah was mistress of the Hermitage; each respected the other's position. When Emily became too ill to preside in Washington, Sarah came to her rescue and served until the end of Jackson's term of office, at which time the family resumed residence at the Hermitage. The beautiful mansion was often crowded with the aging ex-President's faithful supporters, whom she greeted with unfailing courtesy. Sarah and her family were a great comfort to Jackson during his declining years spent in his Tennessee home.

THE GOWN REPRESENTING Sarah Jackson was originally her wedding gown. The tightly fitted bodice is boned and has deep points in both the front and back of the basque waistline with shoe type lacing down the back. The low off-shoulder neckline of the satin bodice is edged with a wide bertha collar of fine lace. The floor length skirt is of embroidered white mull. Six tracings of embroidery about eight inches wide start at the waistline and run down the skirt into a wide embroidered band fourteen inches above the hemline. The heavy white embroidery floss is worked into a delicate rosebud and leaf pattern. The soft ivory gown as we see it today has mellowed from the original traditional white. The back of the hair style features a braided Grecian knot ending in side curls from behind the ears. This figure is one of the smallest in the Collection and shows Sarah Jackson as being very petite and ingénue.

MARTIN VAN BUREN'S wife had passed away seventeen years before his election as President. He moved into the White House with his four unmarried sons, but there was no First Lady. The President's oldest son, Abram, shortly provided a candidate for the vacancy. During the winter of 1837-1838 he met and became engaged to Miss Angelica Singleton who was visiting in Washington from South Carolina. Before she returned home the President asked her to preside as First Lady at the White House after the wedding, which was set for November. Angelica made her first public appearance at the New Year's reception in 1839 and from all accounts performed exceedingly well. After a trip to Europe, where the young couple was entertained by royalty, Angelica sought to introduce some of the more formal customs of European entertaining at the White House; this brought down on her head criticism of those who believed such aristocratic innovations might endanger our democratic form of government. After Van Buren's term ended Angelica and Abram lived with the ex-President, first at Kinderhook, New York, and later in New York City.

THE FIRST APPEARANCE of the hoop skirt is seen in the gown worn by Angelica Van Buren. It is fashioned of heavy piled Lyons type velvet of royal blue and is made in two pieces. The sweeping gored skirt is shirred to a waistband and falls into a full circular train. A wide 18-inch facing finishes the bottom of the skirt which measures ten yards around the hem. The skirt is built over its own hoop and crinoline petticoats which became very popular after being sponsored by the Empress Eugénie. The hoop was then worn by ladies in all walks of life. Tightly fitted, the boned bodice comes to points in the front and back, and extends slightly over the waistline forming a tiny peplum. Extremely low cut, the neckline is off the edge of the shoulder and has only a slight cap sleeve. A wide bertha collar of fine lace around the shoulders softens the neckline. This gown, truly regal in design, is a classic and could be worn during any period and considered stylish.

JANE FINDLAY

MRS. WILLIAM HENRY HARRISON was too ill to go to Washington with her husband for his inauguration in 1841. The newly elected President selected his daughter-in-law, Mrs. Jane Irwin Harrison, to accompany him and act as First Lady until his wife could arrive later in the spring. Young Mrs. Harrison was the niece and adopted daughter of Mrs. James (Jane) Findlay, an old friend of the Harrison family. It was decided that Jane Findlay would go to Washington with young Mrs. Harrison to act as chaperone and assist the younger woman in her duties as First Lady. Jane had formerly lived in Washington as the wife of a Congressman, and so was well versed in the intricacies of social life on "the Hill." General Harrison's death within a month of his inauguration cut short the White House careers of both ladies. The elder Mrs. Harrison had been preparing for the journey to the capital when the shocking news of her husband's death reached her in Ohio.

THE GOWN WORN by Mrs. Findlay at the inaugural ball of President William Henry Harrison is fashioned of dark-brown heavy pile Lyons type velvet. Featuring extremely large puff, or leg-of-mutton sleeves, it is considered a truly American period gown. The short-waisted bodice is fitted tightly and has a wide boat neckline, wl ich is finished with a banding of fine white embroidered muslin, with a squared sca'loped edge. A separate shawl collar covering the back of the neck and shoulders extends over the top of the sleeves, which are shirred at the shoulders and are cuffed with the same white muslin. The skirt is made of many straight widths of velvet gathered at the waistline, falling into rich deep folds. A wide, faced hem gives an elegant finish to the gown which drops evenly to the floor. Around the neck of the figure a large gold locket is worn on a brown velvet ribbon.

JULIA TYLER

ETITIA TYLER was in very poor health when her husband, John Tyler, took office following the death of President Harrison in 1841. She was able to be present at only one White House function—the marriage of her daughter, Elizabeth, on January 31, 1842. Later that year she passed away after a long illness. For almost two years the unmarried daughter, also named Letitia, was official hostess. In 1843 the President became interested in the noted New York belle, Julia Gardiner. Both she and her father were invited to an outing on the U.S.S. Princeton, when during the firing of a salute, an explosion killed several people, among them Mr. Gardiner. President Tyler carried the unconscious Julia off the steamer. There followed an engagement culminating in a secret wedding in New York, disclosed to the public only after the couple left the church where the marriage took place. For the next eight months Julia was First Lady at the White House. She loved her new position and the Executive Mansion was filled with life and gaiety as it had not been since Dolly Madison's time. She took an active part in national politics, eagerly supporting her husband's policies, which included the annexation of Texas. Julia's last official function was a dinner party given for the incoming President and Mrs. Polk.

THE GOWN OF Julia Tyler is fashioned of fine white mull made into a three-tiered skirt which is shirred at the waistline. Each of the tiers is extremely full, hangs rather close to the figure, and is edged with a silver thread embroidery forming a scalloped pattern. Between the three silver bands are delicately embroidered flowers and foliage of silk floss in rainbow colors. The tight, basque bodice is stiffly boned and comes to a slight point over the front of the skirt. The low V-shaped neckline is edged with a narrow band of embroidery, which matches that in the tiers of the skirt and continues down the front of the bodice to the waistline. The waist is bound with a band of matching embroidery. Very short and tightly fitted sleeves are set into the sloped shoulders and are finished with embroidery and ruching of white mull. Time has turned the mull into a mellow ivory. The gown was worn by Julia before she was married to President Tyler, when in 1841 she was presented at the Court of Louis Philippe during a trip abroad.

JULIA TYLER 31

*J*AMES POLK of Tennessee brought to Washington as his First Lady a daughter of the new West, his wife, Sarah Childress Polk. As a young girl she had attended the Moravian seminary at Salem, North Carolina, and the schooling she received there in the "higher branches" made her the first First Lady who could boast of an education acquired in a recognized advanced institution for the education of women. She was intelligent and earnest and showed a greater under-standing of political issues than most of her predecessors. So she played a more important role than merely that of official White House hostess. Indeed, she became her husband's trusted confidante and he highly valued her wise counsels. Sarah, who had had a strict religious upbringing, was something of a Puritan. No refreshments were served at her receptions, and dancing at White House functions was dis-continued. But she was a woman's woman none-the-less, interested in fashions, always beautifully gowned, and a charming hostess. During her regime informal receptions became popular, since they made it possible for many people to meet the President and his wife on an easier footing. Mr. and Mrs. Polk left the White House at the height of their popularity (Polk had declined to run for a second term). James and Sarah returned to their home in Nashville. That same year the ex-President died. His wife outlived him by some forty-two years.

MRS. POLK'S GOWN is the one that she wore to the inaugural ball in 1845. It is made of a fine Ottoman silk brocade, in a delicate shade of periwinkle-blue with a woven poinsettia design, combined with rich blue satin. The tight wasp-waisted bodice comes to a point only in front. The slightly rounded boat neckline extends

to the cap of the shoulder giving a feeling of width. A soft draping at the top of the bodice gives a high bosom effect. A lace jabot falls to one side. The puff sleeves are covered with two flounces of lace matching that of the jabot, and are caught at the edge of the shoulders with satin ribbon bows. The skirt, rather straight in front, is shirred to the back of the waistline giving the appearance of a decided bustle. A ladder-like panel of lace and satin ribbon is worked over an insertion of light blue satin down the front of the skirt, and is caught by blue figured satin ribbon bows at the edges.

W HEN Zachary Taylor went to the White House as President, his wife, Margaret, was not especially pleased with the prospect of becoming First Lady, since social life meant little to her. She had been extremely happy and contented in her little cottage home in Baton Rouge and felt no thrill at the change to the Executive Mansion. Mrs. Taylor let it be known early that their daughter, Betty Taylor Bliss, a recent bride, would be the official hostess in her place. Betty, or "Miss Betty" as she was always known, brought youth and enthusiasm to her new duties and was generally popular. On the Fourth of July, 1850, President Taylor presided over the laying of the cornerstone of the Washington Monument. The heat that day was excessive, and the President, who had survived campaigns against the Seminoles in the steaming Florida swamps, and the torrid temperatures of the Mexican plains during the Mexican War, suffered a fatal sun-stroke. Mrs. Taylor, together with Colonel and Mrs. Bliss, returned first to Kentucky and then to Louisiana, where Mrs. Taylor passed away two years later. During the same year Colonel Bliss died very suddenly and Betty went to live in Virginia, near her friends and relatives. Here she married Philip Dandridge and resumed her leadership in society. After living a long and useful life she died in Winchester, Virginia in 1909.

SINCE THE SEWING machine was invented in 1846, the gown which was worn by Betty Bliss is the last in the Collection to be completely made by hand. It is a typical morning or street dress worn in the late 1840's and is made of spice-colored grenadine with a muted plaid of brown, beige, white, blue, and red. The shoulders of the rounded neckline are covered by a shawl collarette of fine princess lace edged in black velvet ribbon an inch and a half wide, over a self collar of plaid. The

bottoms of the revers are edged with a two-inch fringe, which repeats the colors of the plaid and falls over the cap of the sleeves. Lace and velvet bands cross at the bustline and continue to the waist. The wide-cut bell-shaped elbow-length sleeves, just introduced during this period, have two vertical insertions of plaid and are edged with a plaid binding that is finished with a narrow multi-colored fringe. The voluminous skirt is shirred to the bodice at the natural waistline and is trimmed with two broad flounces, which are bordered with bands of plaid and edged with fringe.

ABIGAIL FILLMORE

*T*HE death of Zachary Taylor promoted Vice-President Millard Fillmore and his wife, Abigail, to the White House in 1850. Mrs. Fillmore had been a school teacher and was accounted something of a bluestocking. She was deeply interested in political affairs. It is said she differed with her husband on the issue of the Fugitive Slave Law. The Fillmore administration represents a rather quiet period in the social life of the Executive Mansion. Abigail was content to spend much of her time with her family. Moreover she was in poor health. So she never got into the full swing of Washington's social activities. Nevertheless, she presided with dignity at all official dinners and receptions, occasionally with the assistance of her daughter, Mary Abigail. Mrs. Fillmore introduced several innovations into the White House. One of these was a bathtub, the first to be installed in the Executive Mansion. Another was a library. When she took up residence in the Executive Mansion she found that there wasn't a single book. As a former school teacher she felt she had to do something to fill this literary void, so Congress made a small appropriation for the books. Abigail Fillmore attended the inaugural of President Pierce on March 4, 1853. The day was very stormy. As a result of exposure to the inclement weather she caught a chill which developed into a serious illness. She died a few weeks later.

THE GOWN ONCE worn by Mrs. Fillmore is fashioned of mauve colored silk taffeta. The low oval neckline is of fine white shirred net which is caught with bands of delicate taffeta tubing following the oval line of the neck. Short cap sleeves are set into the basque bodice, which ends in points over the front and the back of the skirt. The bodice is fastened by a lacing running up the back. Around the shoulders of the figure is a shawl of fine ecru colored lace. The gored skirt is slightly shirred in the back forming a small but definite bustle. An elaborate flounce of embroidered brocade bands the bottom of the skirt and is attached with a narrow taffeta ruffle. The tubing used on the bodice is repeated in the embroidery of the flouncing following the scallop design. The costume is completed with a dainty handkerchief edged with lace, and a wreath of flowers is worn on the head.

JANE PIERCE

*J*ANE PIERCE came to the White House after her husband, Franklin Pierce, was elected to the Presidency in 1852, under tragic circumstances. She had always opposed his entry into politics, and despite the fact that he had served as Representative and Senator she had persuaded him to forsake his political career. Her frail health and the loss of two of her children were factors in Pierce's decision to yield to her pleas. But the Mexican War, in which he fought with distinction, brought Pierce back into public notice. He was nominated for the Presidency and elected by a veritable landslide. But within a few weeks, tragedy again overtook the Pierces. Their only remaining son, Ben, was killed in a train wreck. Jane Pierce, prostrated by grief, did not join her husband in Washington until after the inauguration. Though she carried on bravely as White House hostess, she never recovered from the shock of her terrible loss. Franklin Pierce's single term in office was a stormy one, disturbed by the political controversies that preceded the Civil War. At the end of his term, Jane and he returned to their New Hampshire home.

THIS DULL-BLACK GOWN was worn by Mrs. Pierce while in the White House. It is fashioned of black cotton tulle embroidered with silver dots that have tarnished with time. The black tulle is made over heavy black silk taffeta. The tight basque bodice has a conservative, round neckline and sleeves ending just above the elbow. The full shirred skirt of taffeta is also covered by an overskirt of embroidered tulle. An unusual jacket of the same black tulle, which until inspected closely appears to be a part of the dress, has very large three-quarter length bell sleeves. The V-shaped neckline of this jacket covers the top of the shoulders and is crossed at the waistline in front. A shawl back ends in two long pointed panels which fall into the lower folds of the skirt. Displayed with the gown is a small headdress of lace which is trimmed with dull jet, gold, and velvet.

HARRIET LANE, blond, violet-eyed, an acknowledged beauty, played hostess for her bachelor uncle, James Buchanan, when he came to the White House as President in 1857. She had presided over his home, Wheatlands, and, later, over his establishment when he was American Minister in London. She dined with Queen Victoria and Prince Albert, attended court functions, was presented to Empress Eugénie and Napoleon III. Harriet was thus well prepared for her White House duties. She was very popular with Washington society, and Buchanan's administration was accounted the gayest in many years, contrasting in this respect with the Pierce regime. Then the care-free era ended with John Brown's abortive uprising in 1859. But there was one last social triumph for Harriet, when she presided over the entertainment of the Prince of Wales during his Washington visit in the fall of 1860. After leaving the White House she married, in 1866, wealthy Henry Elliott Johnston of Baltimore. But tragedy dogged her life for the next eighteen years. Death successively claimed her uncle, her two sons and finally her beloved husband. Her memory is perpetuated in the fine art collection she assembled and in the Harriet Lane Wing, her gift to Johns Hopkins Hospital.

THE GOWN of Harriet Lane Johnston is one of the most beautiful in the Collection and is typical of the era it represents. The elegant and simple lines of the gown make it an ageless design that could be worn during any period. The gown was worn by Harriet when she was married in 1866, and is made of an exquisitely water-marked heavy moire. The off-shoulder neckline is beautifully detailed with tiny tucks of French illusion caught to a band of satin with narrow moire tubing. Extending from under the satin shoulder banding is a four-inch flounce of fine lace from under which hang narrow white satin ribbons that fall gracefully over the upper arm. The top of the neckline is framed with the same fine lace. The tight basque bodice is boned and goes into a sharp V-shaped point in front at the waist. Deep pleats at the waistline make the skirt full and soft, and the long sweeping train is elegant indeed. The entire hem of the gown and train is finished with spade-shaped scalloping that is edged with two tiny pipings of satin. A duster ruffle of finely pleated batiste peers from beneath the hemline. At the request of Mrs. Johnston's (Harriet's) family, an exquisite bridal veil of rosepoint lace has been draped over the arms of the figure as a shawl or stole. The entire costume has mellowed to a soft ivory from its original bridal white, but has lost none of its charm and elegance.

*M*ARY TODD LINCOLN is perhaps the most controversial figure among our First Ladies. Had she presided in the White House during an era of peace her official career might have been comparatively untroubled. But she came to Washington when storm clouds were hovering over the nation and she fell victim to wartime rancors. Mary Todd married Lincoln when he was a struggling Illinois attorney, although she numbered among her admirers the already prominent Stephen A. Douglas. She discerned even then in homespun Abraham, the future President. She was ambitious, but when her greatest ambition was realized, she failed to find happiness. A southerner, with members of her family in both the Confederate and Union armies, she was bound to meet hostility, especially on the part of Union supporters. If she gave entertainments, she was accused of frivolity during a national crisis. If she did not, she was accused of failing to lighten the gloom engendered by Confederate victories. The death of her son, Willie, in 1862, plunged her into paroxysms of grief. But there was more tragedy to come. On April 14, 1865, Lincoln was assassinated. Later, in 1871, another son, Tad, died of typhoid. Grief brought her to the verge of madness. A tragic, little understood figure, tried beyond endurance by misfortune!

THE GOWN OF Mrs. Lincoln is made of a heavy Lyons type velvet in a rich shade of royal-purple. The tightly fitted basque bodice has a wide V-shaped neckline draped with a heavy fichu of black Alençon lace which has a dainty white edging. A bouquet of pansies is placed at the bosom. The elbow-length sleeves are puffs of Alençon lace combined with garlands of draped white French illusion, coming

from under the fichu. The boned bodice is deeply pointed over the skirt, and the waistline is piped with a narrow silk cording as are all the seams in the bodice as well as those of the full skirt which is made of ten straight pieces of velvet. The skirt is drawn into the waistline by the use of unpressed pleats. The entire hemline and train is finished with the same white silk piping. On display with the gown is a fan made of purple taffeta and also a small purple parasol which was carried with the gown.

AN assassin's bullet summoned Andrew Johnson to take the Presidency of the United States. Mrs. Johnson, an invalid confined to her room, could not assume the obligations of First Lady. It was decided that their daughter, Martha Johnson Patterson, would preside at the White House instead of her mother. On arriving at the Executive Mansion she found that there was much to be done before any entertaining could take place. The building had suffered during the war years and had to be completely renovated; but with careful attention to the task she was able to have the Mansion in readiness in time for the opening of the social season of 1865. These were trying days in Washington, particularly in the White House. Mrs. Patterson was a person of strong character and stood at her father's side all through the months of the impeachment proceedings, always calm, with never a hint of uncertainty as to the outcome. After the close of her father's administration she returned to the family home in Greeneville, Tennessee.

THIS COSTUME IN the Collection, once belonging to Mrs. Patterson, is not a gown but a cloak, of foreign origin. Introduced to fashion about 1850, this garment was called the "burnous," a cloak worn by the Arabs and Moors. Being extremely voluminous it was the solution to the problem of an outer wrap to be worn gracefully and comfortably over the large hoop skirt. The cloth of this garment is made from a combination of light creamy silk and goat's hair woven closely together. The flowing lines of the cloak are draped on the figure in such a way as to show to advantage the elaborate gold braid motifs in the corners and the braid and tassel edging. The burnous has a gold-tasseled hood, which could be worn up or pushed back at will.

JULIA GRANT

HIS outstanding services to the country during the Civil War assured Ulysses S. Grant of the nomination for the Presidency by the Republicans and his subsequent election. His wife, Julia Dent Grant, faced her new duties as White House hostess with confidence. It is to be assumed that she was delighted to exchange the uncertainties and discomforts of a roving life as wife of an army man for the security and luxury of the Executive Mansion. She·spent much of her time during her husband's two terms in office welcoming groups and delegations of Union veterans calling to pay their respects to their former chief. Julia enjoyed her duties as First Lady and as time passed she became increasingly popular with the American people, despite the political troubles in which her husband was involved. After leaving the White House the Grants made a two years' triumphal trip around the world.

MRS. GRANT WORE this gown to the second inaugural ball in 1873. The regal gown, made of heavy white and silver brocade, presented to her by the Emperor of China, differs from the earlier gowns of the Collection in that it does not have the deeply pointed bodice that was so predominant during the preceding century. The fitted bodice follows the natural waistline of the figure and features a scooped neckline and cap sleeves. Lace and a band of salmon-pink satin frame the neckline. There is also a short jabot of fine ecru colored lace. Covering the shoulders and a portion of the upper arm is an ecru colored lace fichu worn by Mrs. Grant at the first inaugural ball. Again we see the redingote influence in the skirt. Having a peg pleat on either side, it opens down the center front from the waist showing an under skirt of salmon-pink satin with a panel of rosepoint lace heavily jeweled with sequins, pearls, and rhinestones. A short sweeping train is formed by the fullness of the skirt, which is drawn to the back into a small bustle. The waistline of the bodice extends over the bustle in the back and has two folded tabs caught up into a flat bow effect.

LUCY HAYES

*L*UCY WEBB HAYES came to the White House with her husband, Rutherford B. Hayes, in 1877, with considerable experience in official entertaining. She had acted as hostess for her husband when he was in Congress and during his five years as Governor of Ohio. Hayes became President after a bitterly contested election which was finally decided in his favor by a congressional commission. In the ensuing heated political situation, considerable tact was demanded of the new First Lady. She apparently did very well. Mrs. Hayes was the first college graduate to preside in the White House. Her Alma Mater was Wesleyan Female College in Cincinnati. Her wide cultural background won her the admiration of groups with the most different interests which visited the White House. Much of the entertaining had to be official of course, but the celebration of the couple's silver anniversary was a more personal affair. The Hayes' retired to their family home, Spiegel Grove, in Fremont, Ohio, after four years in Washington.

THE VERY ELABORATE gown representing Mrs. Hayes is typical of the fashion during the latter half of the nineteenth century. Heavy ivory satin and rich silk taffeta brocade, with a woven gold thistle rose pattern, are combined to make this gown. The coatlike bodice, pointed in front, is cut into eight pieces in the back tapering at the small waistline and fanning out into a long rounded tail that falls over the train of the skirt. The three-quarter length sleeves are set into narow-width shoulders and have a panel of lace which is heavily worked with pearls. At the bottom of the sleeves are narrow lace ruffles which are caught with flat fan-shaped bows. A wide band of Duchess lace frames the deep V-shaped neckline which is filled in with a crushed tulle scarf. Puffs of satin fall from the front of the waist over the hip and disappear into the coattail of the bodice. The satin skirt has two elaborate bandings of heavy pearl embroidery, above which are flat drapings of satin caught by ribbon rosettes. Fringe of silk and pearls edges the embroidered bands. The hemline in front is tongue-scalloped over satin pleating which continues into the train in back. This gown was worn by Mrs. Hayes at a state dinner honoring the Grand Duke Alexis of Russia on his tour of America.

*J*AMES A. GARFIELD was another of the Civil War Generals to be advanced to a place of political preëminence. After the war he entered the United States Congress and the Garfields moved to Washington from their home in Ohio. It was during this period that Lucretia acquired some familiarity with Washington social life. Both she and her husband (he had once been a college professor) were interested in the ideas and culture of their time, and they naturally attracted people of similar tastes. Mrs. Garfield presided with dignity and grace at all official functions. But fate cut short her career in the White House. On July 2, 1881 only four months after his inauguration, James Garfield was struck down by an assassin's bullet as he was entering the railroad station in Washington. For three months he lingered, Lucretia always at his side, before death came. Mrs. Garfield returned to their home in Mentor, Ohio.

THE LAVISH LAVENDER satin gown worn by Mrs. Garfield has long since mellowed into a soft pearl-gray. This gown has the influence of the waistcoat worn by gentlemen of the Louis period. The fitted bodice is fastened by self-covered buttons to the hipline in front and has a deep keyhole neckline, which is filled in with crushed white illusion. A small standing collar of satin and lace is caught with satin cording ending in a knot of loops at the throat. The diagonal bottom of the jacket is edged with a wide flounce of exquisite Brussels point lace and is drawn back into a large bustle which falls in tapered points onto the train of the skirt. The long fitted sleeves are finished with flounces of Brussels lace which are tied with satin tubing. About the shoulders of the figure has been placed a narrow

scarf of fine lace, and a small nosegay of pansies is nestled at the waist. The satin skirt, being rather straight in front, has two wide flounces of Brussels lace attached by small satin cording tied in front into bows. The sweeping train is edged with puffed ruching of satin. This gown was worn by Mrs. Garfield at the inaugural ball of 1881, which was held in the unfinished Museum building of the Smithsonian, now housing the Collection.

MARY MC ELROY

*A*GAIN a Vice-President was called upon to be President after an assassination. When President Garfield died, Chester Alan Arthur took the oath of office and moved into the White House. His wife's tragic death in 1880 had left him a widower. Now he asked his sister, Mary McElroy, to act as First Lady. She consented and carried through in a charming and dignified manner. Since she was not the wife of the President she was free to come and go, to make private social calls, and accept invitations. President Arthur did not accord her the social precedence of a President's wife, and therefore, according to Washington protocol, it was not necessary to give Mrs. McElroy the position of honor at all social functions. Chester Arthur had always entertained on a lavish scale in private life, and naturally, now, during his term of office, his hospitality was prodigious. Mary McElroy was always at his side, planning and assisting; they both were very popular in Washington. It is said that the White House was never gayer than during this period. The people of Washington felt the loss distinctly when President Arthur and Mrs. McElroy left the Executive Mansion.

MRS. McELROY'S GOWN is made of heavy pearl-gray silk satin damask of an allover morning-glory pattern. The fitted bodice has a wide, sweetheart neckline and slightly puffed sleeves edged in fine eggshell colored lace. A ruffled lace collar covering the shoulders extends to the waistline and is caught at the bosom with a corsage of pink and red carnations. The full gored skirt sweeps the floor with fullness in the back but has no suggestion of the back-swept bustle seen in the preceding gowns. Edging the panel down the front of the skirt is an embroidery of cut steel, seed pearls and tiny French sequins. The embroidery, which repeats the morning-glory pattern of the damask, is continued over the seams of the bodice and on the cuffs of the sleeves. This gown, though simple in design, has an elegance all its own.

FRANCES CLEVELAND

W HEN Grover Cleveland was inaugurated as President in 1885 he was a bachelor, but very soon he and Frances Folsom became secretly engaged. That was in June, of 1885. They were married in the White House one year later. During the first year of his administration his married sister, Rose Elizabeth Cleveland, served as his hostess. All of Washington, not to mention the nation, was excited over the fact that a bride would be First Lady. Frances Folsom Cleveland's youth gave new interest to state entertaining, and her charming personality won her many friends. The Clevelands moved to New York during the Harrison administration but returned in 1893 when Grover Cleveland was reëlected President. Frances Cleveland resumed her duties as First Lady, and the social life that centered around her was again full of gaiety. During the second term the Clevelands had two children, both born in the White House. At the close of the administration the Clevelands retired to their home, Westlands, at Princeton, New Jersey.

THE GOWN REPRESENTING Mrs. Cleveland was worn during her husband's second administration. It is made of chiné satin brocade, originally apple-green in color with vivid pink roses. The material has now faded with time into a deep-ivory, the roses being distinguishable only by their black outline. A pattern of morning-glories woven into the fabric gives a high luster, adding to its richness. The off-shoulder bodice has winged, puff sleeves of brocade with an under sleeve of pink velvet. The bustline of the bodice is draped over a pink velvet corselet that is stiffly boned, with points both in front and back. A flounce of ivory Valenciennes lace covers the top of the sleeves. Velvet bows and gold filigree butterflies sprinkled with sequins are nestled at the bosom and around the shoulders. The full shaped skirt has deep inverted tucks in front and back, but the bustle effect is completely absent. Mrs. Cleveland's dislike of the bustle is said to have had great influence in causing it to lose its popularity and eventually disappear.

*T*HE interim between the two Cleveland administrations brought Benjamin Harrison to the Presidency and Caroline Lavinia Scott Harrison, his wife, to the White House as First Lady. The couple had spent six years in Washington, when Harrison was U. S. Senator from Indiana, and during that time they had become well established in the social and political life of the capital. Actually Mrs. Harrison did not desire further public life after Harrison's term as Senator ended and was happy to retire with him to their home. However, two short years later she found herself again a resident of Washington, this time as First Lady. She entered upon her new career with eagerness and enthusiasm, and her parties, dinners and receptions were brilliant affairs. Late in the winter of 1891-1892 Mrs. Harrison suffered from an attack of grippe, from which she never completely recovered. She died the following fall while still a resident of the White House.

MRS. HARRISON CHOSE for her inaugural ball gown one that was typically American in fabric and design. It was fashioned of heavy silver-gray silk faille and brocade especially woven for her, featuring the bur oaks which grow so profusely in Indiana, President Harrison's home state. The tight, boned basque bodice has a V-shaped neckline with a collar edged with a fringe of silver and gold beads. The three-quarter length sleeve comes from under a shorter draped sleeve and has a soft cotton net sleevette from the elbow finished with a fringe of beads. The basque waistline has a stiffly boned point in front. Four panels of the silvery satin brocade, edged in fringe, form the front of the skirt. Each of these panels has a pleated insertion of apricot satin veiled with lace. The back of the skirt, completely of faille, has deep tucks and falls into a short train. Pearl-gray gloves and gray satin slippers complete the costume.

MARY MC KEE

DURING the illness of her mother, Mrs. Harrison, Mary McKee acted as First Lady. Her two children provided much relaxation and entertainment for their grandparents during their visits to Washington. After her mother's death in 1892, Mary McKee assumed full charge of the household and acted as hostess for the remainder of her father's term. She made a great many friends and performed her official duties with dignity. After leaving the White House she continued to lead a very full life, always interested in social work, and during World War I was actively engaged in relief work.

MRS. McKEE'S GOWN, made of champagne-colored brocade, mustard-colored velvet, and gold-colored satin, is the one that she wore to her father's inaugural ball in 1889. It is a gown typical of the era when the bustle was at its height. The satin brocade, with a woven design of goldenrod in moss-green and gold, blends beautifully with the velvet and satin. The fitted basque bodice has a deep V-shaped neckline edged in heavy scrolls of lace embroidered with silver and amber beads. This neckline is filled in with draped velvet and has a high collar of beaded lace. Underneath the collar hangs a fishnet-like bib of beads which ends in long beaded fringe. The tight elbow-length sleeves are bound by beaded lace scrolls and velvet. The front of the skirt has panels of deeply pleated gold satin which are bound with wide bands of brocade. Over the satin panels at the hipline are scrolls of encrusted lace and fringe. The opening of the redingote-type skirt shows a mustard-colored velvet underskirt. The back of the skirt is made of brocade which is fashioned into a bustle and sweeps into a train. An old gold fan, tan gloves, and tan slippers complete this costume.

IDA MCKINLEY

*A*FTER a successful career in Ohio state politics, William McKinley was inaugurated as President in 1897, and he and his wife, Ida Saxton McKinley, moved to Washington to take up residence in the White House. Mrs. McKinley had been an invalid since 1876 and now was not physically able to assume all of the obligations of the position of First Lady. Consequently social activities at the Executive Mansion were sharply curtailed and simplified. However, she did appear at all state dinners and receptions on the arm of her husband; she never relinquished the prerogatives of her position to anyone else. The President saw to it that every effort was made to safeguard and protect her; he even seated her at his side at social functions rather than in the place normally assigned the First Lady, in order that he might keep a close watch over her to detect the slightest signs of fatigue. In 1901 the McKinleys attended the American Exposition at Buffalo where he planned to make a public appearance. After seeing that Mrs. McKinley was safely on her way home, since crowds were too much for her, he proceeded to the reception in Exposition Hall. It was during this function that he fell victim of an assassin's bullet. After his death Mrs. McKinley returned to their home in Canton, Ohio.

THE GOWN WORN by Mrs. McKinley at the inaugural ball in 1897 is distinctly reminiscent of the gay 90's. It is elaborately fashioned of heavy white satin and priceless lace. The pointed basque has long sleeves that are full above the elbow and are set in sloping shoulders, which are richly decorated with a motif of tiny pearls. A vestee of rose point lace fills in the front of the deep cut bodice, which has a high tight collar edged in a fine ruffle of lace, so typical of that era. Wide lace

revers frame the neckline, and the flounces at the bottom of the sleeves are of the same lace. Five lines of fagoting trace up the back as seams. The skirt is slightly flared at the bottom with a hemline of deep cut rounded scalloping edged with a narrow ruching of lace. A pleated duster is worn underneath. Pearls and rhinestones are used in the heavy embroidery down the front of this skirt, which is framed by an overskirt of rose point lace. A second overskirt of heavy satin falls into a fan-shaped train, which is edged with a ruffle of satin caught intermittently with self-color satin bowknots. A silk gauze fan, embroidered with pearls and with mother-of-pearl studs, finishes the costume.

*T*HEODORE ROOSEVELT was on a mountain hike in the Adirondacks when the news of President McKinley's assassination reached him. He, who had accepted the nomination to the Vice Presidency with reluctance, was now called by fate to the Presidency. He was young and energetic, a believer in the "strenuous" life and his administration provided the press with plenty of news. His wife, Edith Kermit Roosevelt, played her part as First Lady with dignity and grace. Shortly after their arrival the President found it advisable to repair and redecorate the White House which had suffered many changes since it was rebuilt under President Madison. It is easy to imagine the joy with which Edith Roosevelt entered into a round of entertaining in the newly decorated and refurnished mansion. Gone were the reminders of the Victorian period, the 20th century was now at hand; the public was eager to attend White House functions to see what had been accomplished. At the end of his second term the Roosevelts returned to their home, Sagamore Hill.

THE BROCADE IN the gown worn by Mrs. Theodore Roosevelt was especially woven for her, and then the pattern was destroyed. It is made of heavy satin, robin's-egg-blue, with a pattern of gold ostrich plumes in a pinwheel design and tiny swallows in the background. The bodice is slightly long-waisted in front with a three-inch band of satin around the waist. The very simple low square neckline is edged with a rose point lace bertha shirred at the corners. Short sleeves of white French illusion fall softly from under the collar. Six panels form a graceful skirt which has a redingote effect achieved by the use of two deep box pleats on either side of the front of the skirt falling deeply to the hemline. The flared back gores of the skirt fall into a sweeping short train, with a wide hem. This gown was designed especially for the inauguration in 1905. With the gown Mrs. Roosevelt wore a diamond necklace and a blue aigrette in her hair.

*A*FTER a phenomenal rise in politcal power and importance, William Howard Taft was elected President in 1908. He and his family moved into the White House following the inauguration on March 4, 1909. Helen Herron Taft, his wife, had been schooled for years in diplomatic protocol. As "First Lady" of the Philippine Islands she had handled a difficult task with tact and diplomacy. She was able to renew her Washington contacts when her husband was called by President Roosevelt to be his Secretary of War. The White House, while she was First Lady, was the scene of many brilliant affairs, one of the most outstanding being the garden party given to celebrate the presidential couple's silver wedding anniversary. When they left the Executive Mansion in 1913 they did not go into retirement. In 1921 William Howard Taft was appointed Chief Justice of the Supreme Court of the United States, a position he held until his death in 1930. Mrs. Taft survived him by thirteen years and died in her Washington home.

THIS WAS THE first gown to be received by the Smithsonian Institution for its Collection of Dresses of the First Ladies of the White House. It was worn by Mrs. Taft to the inaugural ball held March 4, 1909. Made of sheer white silk chiffon it stresses the Empire waistline which was revived during that year. The neckline of the short bodice is square in front and is deeply V-shaped in back. A ruching of fine ecru lace frames the entire neckline. The bodice is heavily embroidered with silk floss and the goldenrod spray pattern is outlined with a silver thread and crystal beads. The straight cut skirt flares slightly at the hemline and flows into a long sweeping train which falls from the back of the neckline. The embroidered goldenrod pattern is traced throughout the skirt going into a heavier border as it reaches the hemline. Crystal beads and scattered rhinestones give a subtle glitter. A band of crystal beads and rhinestones circles the high waistline. The fabric of this gown was sent to Tokyo by Mrs. Taft to be embroidered especially for her.

ELLEN WILSON

WOODROW WILSON first attained national prominence as President of Princeton University, and then as reform Governor of New Jersey. His election to the Presidency in 1913 was largely due to the split in the Republican ranks caused by the Bull Moose movement. His wife, Ellen Axson Wilson, became First Lady, a position for which she was fully qualified in view of the fact that she had already presided as "First Lady" in the Governor's Mansion in Trenton. Ellen Wilson brought simplicity to the entertaining in the White House, but her charm and cordiality were appreciated by all guests, and this insured the success of her receptions and dinners. The social obligations thrust upon her were too great a burden, however, and in the spring of 1914 she fell ill and passed away the following August.

THE GOWN OF Mrs. Wilson is made of a most unusual fabric. It is fashioned of white silk cut velvet corduroy with a rose pattern. The bodice is long waisted in front and follows the natural waistline in back, and features a wide waistband. The low scooped neckline has a loose fitting over-yoke of silk net which is embroidered with cut steel beads, rhinestones, and various sizes of pearls. This embroidery extends into the elbow length sleeves. Ropes of large pearls are attached to the edge of the sleeves and to the bodice in front and back, and fall into graceful loops over the arms. The peg-top hobble skirt is wrapped around the figure and is shirred up on the left side to permit ease in walking. An underskirt of lace over heavy satin falls from under the softly draped skirt and extends into a long pointed train. This gown typifies the era just before the First World War, and it is interesting to note that this fashion lasted only a short span of years.

EDITH WILSON

*P*RESIDENT WILSON met Mrs. Edith Bolling Galt when she was paying a visit to his cousin, Helen Bones, at the White House, and was immediately attracted to her. During the months that followed their first meeting they became fast friends. As the summer drew to a close, Mrs. Galt finally agreed to permit the announcement of their engagement. They were married in December, 1915. At this time the United States was already threatened with involvement in the war that was raging in Europe, and Edith Wilson, with her devotion and wise counsel, considerably lightened the President's heavy burdens. There was a minimum of entertainment at the Executive Mansion because of the war, especially after our country was involved in it. All Wilson's thoughts and energies were now directed to winning the war and to solving the problems that would arise at the peace conference. Edith accompanied her husband on his two peace missions to Europe. After their return his health broke under the strain of his great responsibilties and, as time went on, he came to rely upon her more and more, not only for companionship, but also for help in his official duties. They retired at the end of the administration to their Washington home where Wilson died three years later. Mrs. Wilson continued to reside in Washington.

THIS GOWN WAS a part of Edith's trousseau when she married President Wilson and was later worn by her during the Peace Conference in Paris. The gown is made of heavy Lyons type black velvet and has a deep square neckline. Tucked black tulle fills in the front of the bodice and narrow straps run over the shoulders forming a vee in front and back. A second strap over the shoulder forms the armhole

into which is set a crushed tulle sleeve falling slightly over the top of the arm. Heavy bands of black sequins and jet beads decorate the bodice from which hang large ropes of jet beads. The loops continue under the arms and are caught at the neckline in the back. To the underarm of the sleeve are attached jet tassels suspended from a black silk cord which hangs well over the hipline. The long black skirt has a knee-length tunic in front which extends into a pointed train in back. A wide band of black sequins and jet hangs from the back of the neckline to the bottom of the skirt in back. The severe black of this gown is unrelieved, with the exception of one band of iridescent sequins which border the jet at the neckline.

EDITH WILSON 69

FLORENCE HARDING

WARREN G. HARDING came to Washington as President in 1921, and his wife, Florence Kling Harding, was established as First Lady of the White House. At the request of the President the usual inaugural parade and ball were dispensed with, and the March 4th ceremonies were limited to the actual inauguration. Florence Harding had for many years been a constant assistant to her husband, first in connection with his newspaper and, later, when he entered political life. The White House, which had been closed to the public not only during the war but also while President Wilson was ill, was now thrown open, and the First Lady began entertaining. She presided over the official gatherings with dignity and insisted on the most formal etiquette at all times. President Harding was accompanied by his wife on many official trips, and she was with him on his tour of Alaska and the Pacific Coast when, in 1923, he died suddenly in San Francisco.

MRS. HARDING WORE this gown to a large reception held in the Pan American Building shortly after the inauguration of her husband. Made of rich white satin which has mellowed to a light ivory, the gown has a low-cut square camisole neckline which is finished with a tiny piping of satin. The bosom is filled in with an insertion of net which is heavily ornamented with Baroque pearls, rhinestones, and crystal beads. Short net sleeves with a fringe of crystal beads are decorated in the same manner as the yoke. There are no seams or darts in the entire front of the gown. This is the first gown in the Collection in which the feet are exposed, heralding the beginning of the short skirts of the 20's. The ankle-length hemline falls into a cowl-like draping at the bottom and is caught up to the waistline in back. A tracing of rhinestones and pearls follows the top of the draping and continues up to the shoulderline. The long pointed train falling from the waist is covered with black net and has a pattern of rhinestones running along the left side. Mrs. Harding requested that after her death the evening wrap of peacock-blue net with a collar of ostrich feathers be added to the gown. The costume is completed by pointed-toed satin pumps with rhinestone buckles.

GRACE COOLIDGE

*C*ALVIN COOLIDGE'S rise to national prominence was comparatively rapid. From his law practice in Northampton he quickly rose through various state offices to be Governor of Massachusetts. Through his successful handling of a difficult situation in his home state, he became popular with his party and was enthusiastically nominated as Vice President on the Harding ticket. Harding's sudden death in 1923 brought Coolidge and his wife, Grace, to the White House. The Coolidge family was in Vermont on vacation when the news of Harding's death reached them, and the oath of office was administered to Calvin Coolidge by his father, a notary public. Grace, the Vermont housewife, quickly adapted herself to the complex responsibilities of her new position. The social life of the Executive Mansion during her regime, though simple, was dignified, and her charm and gaiety, in delightful contrast to the quiet reserve of her husband, captured the affection of Washington society. The death of their promising young son, John, in 1924, brought grief into her life. But she showed a brave front to the world, and when she left the White House in 1929, it was said of her that she had been one of the most popular First Ladies in our history. The Coolidges returned to their Northampton home at the end of his term of office.

THIS GOWN WORN by Mrs. Coolidge is the only sleeveless short gown in the Collection. It is fashioned of transparent silk chiffon velvet in burnt-orange. The neckline is deeply V-shaped and the sleeveless bodice hangs loosely to the hips where it is caught and bloused slightly with a rhinestone belt. The skirt has three circular cut tiers falling from the hips and ending in points in the center front. The neckline, waist, and hems of the tiers all follow the same diagonal line. The long train is attached to the camisole type shoulder straps and forms a deep Vee in the back of the bodice. This panel train flows separately from the gown and ends in a deep point which sweeps nearly four yards from the shoulders. The pumps worn with the gown are of the same burnt-orange velvet and have gold heels and rhinestone buckles. The Pi Beta Phi pin seen on the gown was placed there by Mrs. Coolidge herself. A string of pearls and an exquisite fan of ostrich plumes in colors of peach, rose, and orange complete the costume.

LOU HOOVER

*L*OU HENRY HOOVER was on familiar ground when she entered the impressive portals of the White House. She had been in Washington for eight years with her husband, Herbert Hoover, and during this time he had served as Secretary of Commerce under both Harding and Coolidge. Moreover, she had accompanied him, after their marriage at the turn of the century, on his various missions to all parts of the world. Her special qualifications enabled her to help her husband in ways never before considered possible for the wives of presidents. Mrs. Hoover assumed many of the duties connected with public relations, and in performing them acquitted herself admirably. Entertaining at the White House during the Hoover administration was kept as simple as possible because the country was in the depths of a serious depression. At the end of the administration the Hoovers retired to their Palo Alto home.

MRS. HOOVER'S GOWN is fashioned of lustrous pale ice-green silk satin. The deep cowl neckline is caught at each shoulder with small rhinestone clips which are the only ornamentation. Softly draped cape sleeves extend into a capelet across the back which falls into a point below the waistline. Satin cording is used to bind the low waistline of the bias-cut bodice. The long tunic which has a handrolled handkerchief hem falls gracefully into four deep points over the skirt. The full bias skirt hangs softly to the floor and sweeps into a graceful fan-shaped train. The gown is decidedly Grecian in feeling.

ELEANOR ROOSEVELT

$\mathcal{F}$RANKLIN DELANO ROOSEVELT was elected President in 1933 and came to Washington with his wife, Anna Eleanor Roosevelt, to start an administration which was to become the longest ever served by any President of the United States. Eleanor Roosevelt had been of constant assistance. to her husband, especially in the period following his illness in 1921. While she was First Lady she traveled to every section of the country and became familiar with all types of social conditions. Her reports and counsel assisted the President in his program of social reform. But she did not neglect her duties as First Lady, and until the war curtailed such activities, she presided at many teas, dinners, and receptions. Mrs. Roosevelt's charm as well as that of her husband had a certain quality about it that few could resist. During the war all efforts were turned toward its successful prosecution, and little or no entertaining was done in the White House. However, during this period, Mrs. Roosevelt entertained many military and political leaders in the Executive Mansion but always on a simple scale. On one occasion at Hyde Park during the visit of the King and Queen of England, an *al fresco* luncheon of sausages on rolls was served. After her husband's death in 1945, Eleanor returned to Hyde Park, but she did not go into retirement. For anyone of her temperament and ability who has led such a full life this would not have been possible.

MRS. ROOSEVELT'S THIRD inaugural ball gown is made of a warmly tinted silk satin with highlights changing from ivory to deep peach. The bodice has a wide sweetheart neckline and short sleeves which are intricately cut so as to cross over the upper arm. A pattern embroidered with tinted seed pearls edges the neckline and follows the bottom of the sleeves. The beltless bodice extends to a low point from the waistline into the front of the skirt. In the center front seam of the bias-cut skirt is a soft cowl draping. The train which begins at the shoulder falls gracefully into the folds of the skirt.

ELEANOR ROOSEVELT 77

*T*HE death of Franklin Delano Roosevelt brought to the White House the Vice President, Harry S. Truman, and his wife, Bess Wallace Truman. Since her husband had served two terms in the U. S. Senate, as well as Vice President, Mrs. Truman was familiar with Washington official society and its attendant procedures. This was a definite asset when she was called upon to take over as First Lady. Everyone who had occasion to be present at one of the many official functions was duly impressed with her sincere graciousness and charm. During the Truman administration it was decided that a major renovation of the White House should be undertaken. The Blair House, across the street, was occupied by the family while this work was being accomplished. Social affairs were somewhat curtailed during this time because of the limited space. It was here that the attempt on Mr. Truman's life was made in November, 1950. The Trumans were able to move back into the completely renovated White House in the Spring of 1952. The election of November 1952 brought to the Presidency an outstanding military leader, General Dwight D. Eisenhower.

MRS. TRUMAN'S GOWN is floor length and is made of dark elephant-gray silk brocade with a woven design of gold ostrich plumes. Eight handmade leaves of the brocade are placed around the edge of the slightly scalloped V-neckline. Tiny delicate stems made of brocade tubing finish the design. The deep-cut three-quarter length sleeves are set into the fitted bodice and crush slightly at the elbow. The circular skirt falls in soft folds from the hipline to the floor. Mrs. Truman made a good selection in contributing this particular gown to the Collection as it slightly resembles some of those seen earlier in the series in that it is made of heavy rich brocade, and is elegant in feeling, though without any definite styling.